# HEARTLAND BAKING

ALL-AMERICAN CAKES, COOKIES, PIES AND PASTRIES, BREADS AND BARS

# HEARTLAND BAKING

**ALL-AMERICAN CAKES, COOKIES, PIES AND PASTRIES, BREADS AND BARS**

**CONSULTANT EDITOR: LINDLEY BOEGEHOLD**

This edition published in 1995 by
SMITHMARK Publishers Inc.
16 East 32nd Street
New York, NY 10016

SMITHMARK books are available for bulk purchase for sales promotion and for premium use. For details write or call the Manager of Special Sales, SMITHMARK Publishers Inc., 16 East 32nd Street, New York, NY, 10016; (212) 532-6600.

ISBN 0 8317 7454 1

*Publisher:* Joanna Lorenz
*Editorial Manager:* Helen Sudell
*Designer:* Nigel Partridge
*Photographer:* Amanda Haywood and David F. Wisse, Picture Perfect USA (p 6/7)
*Illustrations by:* Estelle Corke
*Recipes by:* Patricia Lousada

Printed and bound in Singapore

# Contents

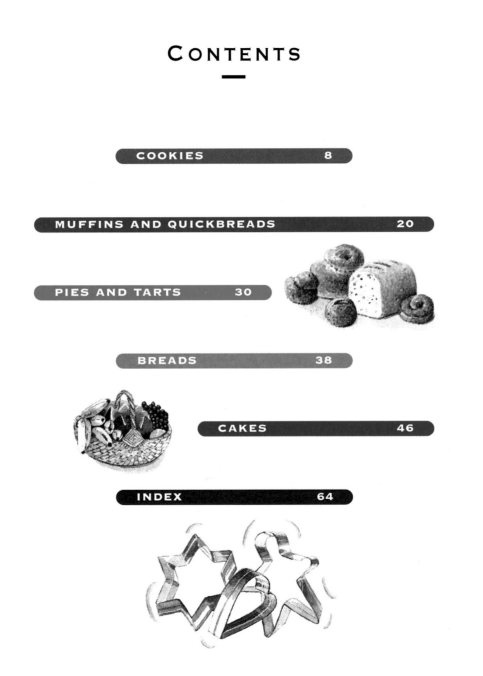

"They're eatin' cream puffs!" cried Hot Biscuit Slim.

Cream Puff Fatty could not believe it, but a thrill of hope urged him to see for himself. True enough, the loggers were tackling the pastries at last. On each plate cream puffs the size of squashes lay in golden mounds . . . They had now stayed four times as long as usual at the table. Other enchantments still kept them in their seats: lemon pies with airy frostings, yellow pumpkin pies strewn with brown spice specks, cherry pies with cracks in their crusts through which the red fruit winked, custard pies with russet freckles on their cobblers, chocolate puddings, glittering cakes of many colors, slabs of gingerbread, sugar-powdered jelly rolls . . . So endearing were the flavors of these pastries that the loggers consumed them all.

From *Paul Bunyan*
by James Stevens, 1892

# RASPBERRY SANDWICH COOKIES

—

THESE PRETTY FRUIT COOKIES ARE MINI VERSIONS OF THE CLASSIC AUSTRIAN LINZER TORTE. IF
YOU FIND RASPBERRY SEEDS INDIGESTIBLE YOU CAN USE SEEDLESS JAM INSTEAD.

**MAKES 32**

*1 cup blanched almonds*

*1½ cups flour*

*¾ cup (1½ sticks) butter, at room temperature*

*½ cup sugar*

*grated rind of 1 lemon*

*1 teaspoon vanilla extract*

*1 egg white*

*⅛ teaspoon salt*

*⅓ cup slivered almonds*

*1 cup raspberry jam*

*1 tablespoon fresh lemon juice*

Place the blanched almonds and 3 tablespoons of the flour in a food processor, blender, or nut grinder and process until finely ground. Set aside.

With an electric mixer, cream the butter and sugar together until light and fluffy. Stir in the lemon rind and vanilla. Add the ground almonds and remaining flour and mix well to form a dough. Gather into a ball, wrap in wax paper, and refrigerate for at least 1 hour.

Preheat oven to 325°F. Line 2 cookie sheets with wax paper.

Divide the dough into 4 equal parts. Working with one section of the dough at a time, roll out to a thickness of ⅛ inch on a lightly-floured surface. With a 2½-inch fluted pastry cutter, stamp out circles. Gather the dough scraps, roll out, and stamp out more circles. Repeat with the remaining dough.

With the small end of a piping tip, or with a ¾-inch cutter, stamp out the centers from half the circles. Place dough rings and circles ½ inch apart on the prepared sheets.

Whisk the egg white with the salt until just frothy. Chop the slivered almonds. Brush only the cookie rings with the egg white, then sprinkle over the almonds. Bake until very lightly browned, 12-15 minutes. Let cool for a few minutes on the sheets before transferring to a rack.

In a saucepan, melt the jam with the lemon juice until it comes to a simmer. Brush the jam over the cookie circles and sandwich together with the rings. Store in an airtight container with sheets of wax paper between the layers.

# CINNAMON REFRIGERATOR COOKIES

CHILLING THE DOUGH ALLOWS THESE COOKIES TO BE SLICED VERY THINLY FOR OPTIMUM CRISPNESS. THEY ARE PERFECT TEA-TIME TREATS.

10

**MAKES 50**

*2⅛ cups flour*

*½ teaspoon salt*

*2 teaspoons ground cinnamon*

*1 cup (2 sticks) unsalted butter, at room temperature*

*1 cup sugar*

*2 eggs*

*1 teaspoon vanilla extract*

In a bowl, sift together the flour, salt, and cinnamon. Set aside.

With an electric mixer, cream the butter until soft. Add the sugar and continue beating until the mixture is light and fluffy.

Beat the eggs and vanilla, then gradually stir into the butter mixture.

Stir in the dry ingredients.

Divide the dough into 4 parts, and roll each into 2-inch diameter logs. Wrap tightly in foil (see left) and refrigerate or freeze until firm.

Preheat the oven to 375°F. Grease 2 cookie sheets with a little butter.

With a sharp knife, cut the dough into ¼-inch slices. Place the rounds on the prepared sheets and bake until lightly colored, about 10 minutes. With a metal spatula, transfer to a rack to cool.

---

### COOK'S TIP

WHEN BAKING COOKIES, IT IS IMPORTANT TO USE HEAVY BAKING SHEETS THAT WON'T BUCKLE IN THE HEAT. THIS ENSURES THE COOKIES DO NOT SLIDE TOGETHER IN THE OVEN. IT IS ALSO BETTER TO BAKE ONE SHEET OF COOKIES AT A TIME TO ENSURE AN EVEN TEMPERATURE.

# GINGER COOKIES

—

THE SPICY FLAVOR OF THESE COOKIES MAKE THEM A FAVORITE WINTER TREAT WITH
HOT CHOCOLATE.

**12**

**MAKES 36**

*1 cup granulated sugar*

*½ cup light brown sugar, firmly packed*

*½ cup (1 stick) butter, at room temperature*

*½ cup (1 stick) margarine, at room temperature*

*1 egg*

*⅓ cup molasses*

*2¼ cups flour*

*2 teaspoons ground ginger*

*½ teaspoon grated nutmeg*

*1 teaspoon ground cinnamon*

*2 teaspoons baking soda*

*½ teaspoon salt*

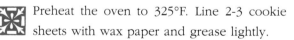 Preheat the oven to 325°F. Line 2-3 cookie sheets with wax paper and grease lightly.

With an electric mixer, cream ½ cup of the granulated sugar, the brown sugar, butter, and margarine until light and fluffy. Add the egg and continue beating to blend well. Add the molasses.

Sift the dry ingredients 3 times, then stir into the butter mixture. Refrigerate for 30 minutes.

Place the remaining sugar in a shallow dish. Roll tablespoonfuls of the dough into balls, then roll the balls in the sugar to coat.

Place the balls 2 inches apart on the prepared sheets and flatten slightly. Bake until golden around the edges but soft in the middle, 12-15 minutes. Let stand for 5 minutes and transfer to a rack to cool.

---

**VARIATION**

TO MAKE GINGERBREAD MEN, INCREASE THE AMOUNT OF FLOUR BY ¼ CUP. ROLL OUT THE DOUGH AND CUT OUT SHAPES WITH A SPECIAL CUTTER. DECORATE WITH ICING, IF WISHED.

# CHOCOLATE ALMONDS

—

**MAKES 36**

*3 tablespoons butter*

*½ cup whipping cream*

*⅔ cup sugar*

*1½ cups sliced almonds*

*¼ cup candied orange peel, finely chopped*

*2 tablespoons candied cherries, chopped*

*½ cup flour, sifted*

*8 1-ounce squares semisweet chocolate*

*1 teaspoon vegetable oil*

 Preheat the oven to 350°F. Grease 2 cookie sheets with a little butter.

Melt the butter, cream, and sugar together and slowly bring to the boil. Take off the heat and blend in the almonds, orange peel, cherries, and flour.

Drop teaspoonfuls of the batter 1-2 inches apart on the prepared sheets and flatten with a fork.

Bake until the cookies brown at the edges, about 10 minutes. Remove from the oven and correct the shape by quickly pushing in any thin uneven edges with a knife or a round cookie cutter. Work fast or they will cool and harden while still on the sheets. If necessary, return to the oven for a few moments to soften. While still hot, use a metal spatula to transfer the cookies to a clean, flat surface.

Melt the chocolate in the top of a double boiler or in a heatproof bowl set over a pan of hot water. Add the oil and stir to blend.

With a metal spatula, spread the smooth underside of the cooled cookies with a thin coating of the melted chocolate.

When the chocolate is about to set, draw a serrated knife across the surface with a slight sawing motion to make wavy lines. Store in an airtight container in a cool place.

# PECAN BARS

—

THESE RICH PASTRY BARS HAIL FROM THE SOUTH, WHERE PECANS GO INTO JUST ABOUT
EVERYTHING. THEY ARE ESPECIALLY GOOD WITH TWO FINGERS OF SOUR MASH BOURBON AS
AN AFTER DINNER TREAT.

14

### MAKES 36

*2 cups flour*

*pinch of salt*

*½ cup granulated sugar*

*1 cup (2 sticks) cold butter or margarine, cut in
  pieces*

*1 egg*

*finely grated rind of 1 lemon*

### FOR THE TOPPING

*¾ cup (1½ sticks) butter*

*¼ cup honey*

*¼ cup granulated sugar*

*¾ cup dark brown sugar, firmly packed*

*5 tablespoons whipping cream*

*4 cups pecan halves*

 Preheat the oven to 375°F. Lightly grease a 15½- x 10½- x 1-inch jelly roll pan.

For the crust, sift the flour and salt into a mixing bowl. Stir in the sugar. With a pastry blender, cut in the butter or margarine until the mixture resembles coarse crumbs. Add the egg and lemon rind and carefully blend with a fork until the mixture just holds together.

Spoon the mixture into the prepared pan. With floured fingertips, press into an even layer. Prick the pastry all over with a fork and refrigerate for 10 minutes.

Bake the pastry crust for 15 minutes. Remove the pan from the oven, but keep the oven on while making the topping.

Melt the butter, honey, and both sugars. Bring to a boil. Boil, without stirring, for 2 minutes. Off the heat, stir in the cream and pecans. Pour over the crust, return to the oven and bake for 25 minutes.

When cool, run a knife around the edge. Invert onto a baking sheet, place another sheet on top and invert again. Dip a sharp knife into very hot water and cut into squares for serving.

---

### COOK'S TIP

IF YOU DON'T HAVE A PASTRY BLENDER, 2 KNIVES WILL
DO THE JOB JUST AS WELL.

---

# CHOCOLATE CHIP BROWNIES

CHOCOLATE CHIPS GIVE THESE CLASSIC DESSERT SQUARES EXTRA FUDGINESS. ALL THEY NEED TO ATTAIN PERFECTION IS AN ICY GLASS OF MILK ON THE SIDE.

**MAKES 24**

*4 1-ounce squares unsweetened chocolate*
*½ cup (1 stick) butter*
*3 eggs*
*1½ cups sugar*
*1 teaspoon vanilla extract*
*pinch of salt*
*¾ cup flour*
*1 cup chocolate chips*

Preheat the oven to 350°F. Line a 13- x 9-inch pan with wax paper and grease.

Melt the chocolate and butter in the top of a double boiler, or in a heatproof bowl set over a pan of gently simmering water (see above right).

Beat together the eggs, sugar, vanilla, and salt. Stir in the chocolate mixture. Sift over the flour and gradually fold in. Add the chocolate chips.

Pour the batter into the prepared pan and spread evenly. Bake until just set, about 30 minutes. Do not overbake; the brownies should be slightly moist inside. Cool in the pan.

To unmold, run a knife all around the edge and invert onto a cookie sheet. Remove the paper. Place a sheet on top and invert again so the brownies are right-side up. Cut into squares for serving.

# APRICOT BARS

—

18

### MAKES 12

*½ cup light brown sugar, firmly packed*
*¾ cup flour*
*6 tablespoons cold unsalted butter, cut into pieces*

### FOR THE TOPPING

*1 cup dried apricots*
*1 cup water*
*grated rind of 1 lemon*
*⅓ cup granulated sugar*
*2 teaspoons cornstarch*
*½ cup walnuts, chopped*

Preheat the oven to 350°F.

In a bowl, combine the brown sugar and flour. With a pastry blender, cut in the butter until the mixture resembles coarse crumbs.

Transfer to an 8-inch square baking pan and press into an even layer. Bake for 15 minutes. Remove from the oven but leave the oven on. Meanwhile, for the topping, combine the dried apricots and water in a saucepan and simmer until soft, about 10 minutes. Strain the liquid and reserve. Chop the apricots.

Return the apricots to the saucepan and add the lemon rind, granulated sugar, cornstarch, and 4 tablespoons of the soaking liquid. Cook for 1 minute, being careful not to go over time.

Cool slightly before spreading the topping over the base (see below). Sprinkle over the walnuts and continue baking for 20 minutes more. Let cool in the pan before cutting into bars.

# APPLE CRANBERRY MUFFINS

—

THESE TART, FRUITY MUFFINS TASTE BEST IN THE FALL WHEN APPLES AND CRANBERRIES ARE JUST PICKED.

20

**MAKES 12**

*4 tablespoons butter or margarine*

*1 egg*

*½ cup sugar*

*grated rind of 1 large orange*

*½ cup fresh orange juice*

*1 cup flour*

*1 teaspoon baking powder*

*½ teaspoon baking soda*

*1 teaspoon ground cinnamon*

*½ teaspoon grated nutmeg*

*½ teaspoon ground allspice*

*¼ teaspoon ground ginger*

*¼ teaspoon salt*

*1-2 apples*

*1 cup cranberries*

*½ cup walnuts, chopped*

*confectioners' sugar, for dusting (optional)*

Preheat the oven to 350°F. Grease a 12-cup muffin pan or use paper liners.

Melt the butter or margarine over a gentle heat. Set aside to cool.

Place the egg in a mixing bowl and whisk lightly. Add the melted butter or margarine and whisk to combine, about 5 minutes.

Add the sugar, orange rind, and juice. Whisk to blend, then set aside.

In a large bowl, sift together the flour, baking powder, baking soda, cinnamon, nutmeg, allspice, ginger and salt. Set aside.

Quarter, core, and peel the apples. With a sharp knife, chop in a coarse dice to obtain 1¼ cups.

Make a well in the dry ingredients and pour in the egg mixture. With a large spoon, stir together until just blended.

Add the apples, cranberries, and walnuts and again stir to blend.

Fill the cups three-quarters full and bake until the tops spring back when touched lightly, 25-30 minutes. Transfer to a rack to cool. Dust with confectioners' sugar, if desired.

---

**VARIATION**

BLUEBERRIES AND BLACKBERRIES MAKE EXCELLENT ALTERNATIVES IF YOU GET AN URGE TO BAKE FRUIT MUFFINS EARLIER IN THE SUMMER.

# RAISIN BRAN MUFFINS

―

THESE HEARTY MUFFINS TASTE SO GOOD IT IS HARD TO BELIEVE THAT THEY ARE GOOD FOR YOU — BUT THEY ARE. DOLLOP A FRUIT SPREAD ON TOP FOR A GUILT-FREE BREAKFAST.

22

**MAKES 15**

*4 tablespoons butter or margarine*
*⅔ cup all-purpose flour*
*½ cup whole-wheat flour*
*1½ teaspoons baking soda*
*⅛ teaspoon salt*
*1 teaspoon ground cinnamon*
*½ cup bran*
*½ cup raisins*
*⅓ cup dark brown sugar, firmly packed*
*¼ cup granulated sugar*
*1 egg*
*1 cup buttermilk*
*juice of ½ lemon*

Preheat the oven to 400°F. Grease 15 muffin cups or use paper liners.

Place the butter or margarine in a saucepan and melt over gentle heat. Set aside.

In a mixing bowl, sift together the all-purpose flour, whole-wheat flour, baking soda, salt, and cinnamon.

Add the bran, raisins, and sugars and blend

together (see below).

In another bowl, mix together the egg, buttermilk, lemon juice, and melted butter.

Add the buttermilk mixture to the dry ingredients and stir lightly and quickly just until moistened; do not mix until smooth.

Spoon the batter into the prepared muffin cups, filling them almost to the top. Half-fill any empty cups with water.

Bake until golden, 15-20 minutes. Serve warm or at room temperature.

# CHEESE MUFFINS

—

SHARP CHEDDAR CHEESE FLAVORS THESE SAVORY MORSELS. THEY ARE EQUALLY AT EASE WITH EGGS AND BACON AT BREAKFAST, TOMATO SOUP FOR LUNCH, OR ACCOMPANYING ROAST CHICKEN FOR DINNER.

24

**MAKES 9**

4 tablespoons butter

1½ cups flour

2 teaspoons baking powder

2 tablespoons sugar

¼ teaspoon salt

1 teaspoon paprika

2 eggs

½ cup milk

1 teaspoon dried thyme

2 ounces sharp cheddar cheese, cut into ½ inch
   dice

Preheat the oven to 375°F. Thickly grease 9 muffin cups with butter. If you do not have muffin cups use paper liners.

Melt the butter and set aside.

In a mixing bowl, sift together the flour, baking powder, sugar, salt, and paprika.

In another mixing bowl, combine the eggs, milk, melted butter, and thyme, and whisk to blend.

Slowly add the milk mixture to the dry ingredients and stir just until

moistened, taking care not to mix until smooth.

Place a heaped spoonful of batter into the prepared cups. Drop a few pieces of cheese over each, then top with another spoonful of batter (see above). For an all-round, even baking, half-fill any empty muffin cups with water.

Bake the muffins until puffed and golden, approximately 25 minutes.

Let stand 5 minutes before unmolding onto a cooling rack.

Serve warm or at room temperature.

# LEMON WALNUT BREAD

—

FRUIT AND NUT LOAVES HAVE BECOME TEA-TIME STAPLES. THIS TANGY BREAD MAKES A TASTY
SANDWICH WHEN SPREAD WITH CREAM CHEESE.

**MAKES 1 LOAF**

*½ cup (1 stick) butter or margarine, at room*
    *temperature*
*½ cup sugar*
*2 eggs, at room temperature, separated*
*grated rind of 2 lemons*
*2 tablespoons fresh lemon juice*
*1½ cups cake flour*
*2 teaspoons baking powder*
*½ cup milk*
*½ cup walnuts, chopped*
*⅛ teaspoon salt*

Preheat the oven to 350°F. Line the bottom and sides of a 9- x 5-inch loaf pan with wax paper and grease.

With an electric mixer, cream the butter or margarine with the sugar until light and fluffy.

Beat in the egg yolks.

Add the lemon rind and juice and stir until blended. Set aside.

In another bowl, sift together the flour and baking powder, 3 times. Fold into the butter mixture in 3 batches, alternating with the milk. Fold in the walnuts. Set aside.

Beat the egg whites and salt until stiff peaks form. Fold a large dollop of the egg whites into the walnut mixture to lighten it. Fold in the remaining egg whites carefully just until blended.

Pour the batter into the prepared pan and bake until a cake tester inserted in the center of the loaf comes out clean, 45-50 minutes (see below). Stand 5 minutes before unmolding onto a rack to cool.

# BLUEBERRY STREUSEL BREAD

THE CRUMBLY TOP OF THIS FRUIT BREAD IS CALLED A STREUSEL AND DRAWS FROM THE
RICH CULINARY HERITAGE OF AUSTRIA. IT MAKES AN ELEGANT BREAKFAST CAKE TOPPED WITH
A SPOONFUL OF YOGURT.

**MAKES 8 PIECES**

4 tablespoons butter or margarine, at room
    temperature

¾ cup sugar

1 egg, at room temperature

½ cup milk

2 cups flour

2 teaspoons baking powder

½ teaspoon salt

2 cups fresh blueberries

**FOR THE TOPPING**

½ cup sugar

⅓ cup flour

½ teaspoon ground cinnamon

4 tablespoons butter, cut in pieces

 Preheat the oven to 375°F. Grease a 9-inch square baking dish.

With an electric mixer, cream the butter or margarine with the sugar until light and fluffy. Add the egg, beat to combine, then mix in the milk until blended.

Sift the baking powder and salt over the flour, and stir just enough to blend the ingredients.

Add the blueberries and stir.

Transfer to the baking dish.

For the topping, place the sugar, flour, cinnamon, and butter in a mixing bowl. Cut in with a pastry blender or 2 knives until the mixture resembles coarse crumbs.

Sprinkle the topping evenly over the batter in the pan (see above).

Bake until a cake tester inserted in the center comes out clean, about 45 minutes.

Serve warm or cold.

# PEACH LEAF PIE

—

MAKE THIS PIE IN THE SUMMER WHEN PEACHES ARE RIPE. TRADITIONALLY FRUIT PIES WERE SERVED AT HUGE BREAKFASTS TO THE HIRED HANDS WHO CAME TO PICK CROPS ON THE BIG FARMS IN THE MIDWEST. HOWEVER THEY TASTE VERY GOOD EVEN IF YOU HAVE JUST ROLLED OUT OF BED.

30

**SERVES 8**

2½ pounds ripe peaches
juice of 1 lemon
½ cup sugar
3 tablespoons cornstarch
¼ teaspoon grated nutmeg
½ teaspoon ground cinnamon
2 tablespoons butter, diced

**FOR THE CRUST**

2 cups flour
¾ teaspoon salt
½ cup (1 stick) cold butter, cut in pieces
3 tablespoons cold shortening, cut in pieces
5-6 tablespoons ice water
1 egg beaten with 1 tablespoon water, for glazing

For the crust, sift the flour and salt into a bowl. Add the butter and shortening and cut in with a pastry blender until the mixture resembles coarse crumbs.

With a fork, stir in just enough water to bind the dough. Gather into 2 balls, one slightly larger than the other. Wrap in wax paper and refrigerate for at least 20 minutes.

Place a baking sheet in the oven and preheat to 425°F.

Drop a few peaches at a time into boiling water for 20 seconds, then transfer to a bowl of cold water. When cool, peel off the skins.

Slice the peaches and combine with the lemon juice, sugar, cornstarch, and spices. Set aside.

On a lightly-floured surface, roll out the larger dough ball about ⅛ inch thick. Transfer to a 9-inch pan and trim the edge. Refrigerate.

Roll out the remaining dough ¼ inch thick. Cut out leaf shapes 3 inches long, using a template if needed. Mark veins with a knife. With the scraps, roll a few balls.

Brush the bottom of the pie shell with egg glaze. Add the peaches, piling them higher in the center. Dot with the butter.

To assemble, start from the outside edge and cover the peaches with a ring of leaves. Place a second ring of leaves above, staggering the positions. Continue with rows of leaves until covered. Place the balls in the center. Brush with glaze.

Bake for 10 minutes. Lower the heat to 350°F and continue to bake for 35-40 minutes more.

# MAPLE WALNUT PIE

—

IN THE MIDWEST WALNUT GROVES WERE GIVEN AS BRIDES' DOWRIES, SUCH WAS THE VALUE OF
THE DENSE AND BEAUTIFUL WOOD. COOKS DEVISED MANY WAYS TO PREPARE THE TREES' HARVEST
OF NUTS, AND THIS MAPLE PIE IS ONE OF THE BEST.

**SERVES 8**

*3 eggs*

*⅛ teaspoon salt*

*¼ cup granulated sugar*

*4 tablespoons butter or margarine, melted*

*1 cup pure maple syrup*

*1 cup walnuts, chopped*

*whipped cream, for decorating*

**FOR THE CRUST**

*½ cup all-purpose flour*

*½ cup whole-wheat flour*

*⅛ teaspoon salt*

*4 tablespoons cold butter, cut in pieces*

*3 tablespoons cold shortening, cut in pieces*

*1 egg yolk*

*2-3 tablespoons ice water*

For the crust, mix the flours and salt in a bowl. Add the butter and shortening and cut in with a pastry blender until the mixture resembles coarse crumbs. With a fork, stir in the egg yolk and just enough water to bind the dough.

Gather into a ball, wrap in wax paper, and refrigerate for 20 minutes.

Preheat the oven to 425°F.

On a lightly-floured surface, roll out the dough about ⅛ inch thick and transfer to a 9-inch pie pan. Trim the edge. To decorate, roll out the trimmings. With a small heart-shaped cutter, stamp out enough hearts to go around the rim of the pie. Brush the edge with water, then arrange the dough hearts evenly around.

Prick the bottom with a fork. Line with crumpled wax paper and fill with pie weights. Bake 10 minutes. Remove the paper and weights and continue baking until golden brown, 3-6 minutes more.

In a bowl, whisk eggs, salt, and sugar together. Stir in the butter or margarine and maple syrup.

Set the pie shell on the baking sheet. Pour in the filling, then sprinkle the nuts generously over the top.

Bake until the pie is just set, about 35 minutes. Allow to cool. Decorate with whipped cream if wished.

# BLUEBERRY PIE

---

IF YOU CAN LAY YOUR HANDS ON SOME HUCKLEBERRIES TRY THIS RECIPE USING THEM.
THE TINY WILD COUSINS OF DOMESTIC BLUEBERRIES MAKE A SUPERB PIE, ALTHOUGH DOMESTIC
BLUEBERRIES ARE PRETTY FABULOUS THEMSELVES.

### SERVES 8

*1 pound blueberries*
*½ cup sugar*
*3 tablespoons cornstarch*
*2 tablespoons fresh lemon juice*
*2 tablespoons butter, diced*

### FOR THE CRUST

*2 cups flour*
*¾ teaspoon salt*
*½ cup (1 stick) cold butter, cut in pieces*
*3 tablespoons cold shortening, cut in pieces*
*5-6 tablespoons ice water*
*1 egg beaten with 1 tablespoon water, for glazing*

For the crust, sift the flour and salt into a bowl. Add the butter and shortening and cut in with a pastry blender until the mixture resembles coarse crumbs. With a fork, stir in just enough water to bind the dough. Gather into 2 equal balls, wrap in wax paper, and refrigerate for 20 minutes.

On a lightly-floured surface roll out 1 dough ball about ⅛ inch thick. Transfer to a 9-inch pie pan and trim to leave a ½-inch overhang. Brush the bottom with egg glaze.

Mix all the filling ingredients together, except the butter (reserve a few blueberries for decoration). Spoon into the shell and dot with the butter. Brush the egg glaze on the edge of the lower crust.

Place a baking sheet in the center of the oven and preheat to 425°F.

Roll out the remaining dough on a baking tray lined with wax paper. With a serrated pastry wheel,

cut out 24 thin strips of dough. Roll out the scraps and cut out leaf shapes for the top of the pie. Mark veins in the leaves with the point of a knife.

Weave the strips in a close lattice, then transfer to the pie using the wax paper. Press the edges to seal and trim. Decorate the pie by arranging the dough leaves around the rim. Brush with egg glaze.

Place in the top half of the oven and bake for 10 minutes. Reduce the heat to 350°F and bake until the pastry is golden, 40-45 minutes more.

Decorate with the reserved blueberries.

# CHOCOLATE LEMON TART

— 

**THIS TART IS A TWIST ON THE CLASSIC FLAVOR COMBINATION OF ORANGE AND CHOCOLATE.**

36

**SERVES 8-10**

*1¼ cups granulated sugar*

*6 eggs*

*grated rind of 2 lemons*

*⅔ cup fresh lemon juice*

*⅔ cup whipping cream*

*chocolate curls, for decorating*

**FOR THE CRUST**

*1¼ cups flour*

*2 tablespoons unsweetened cocoa powder*

*4 tablespoons confectioners' sugar*

*½ teaspoon salt*

*½ cup (1 stick) butter or margarine*

*1 tablespoon water*

Grease a 10-inch tart pan.

For the crust, sift the flour, cocoa powder, confectioners' sugar, and salt into a bowl. Set aside.

Melt the butter and water over low heat. Pour over the flour mixture and stir until the dough is smooth and the flour has absorbed all the liquid.

Press the dough evenly over the base and sides of the prepared tart pan. Refrigerate the tart shell while preparing the filling.

Place a baking sheet in the center of the oven and preheat to 375°F.

Whisk the sugar and eggs until the sugar is dissolved. Add the lemon rind and juice and mix well. Add the cream. Taste the mixture and add more lemon juice or sugar if needed. It should taste tart but also sweet.

Pour the filling into the tart shell and bake on the hot sheet until the filling is set, 20-25 minutes. Allow to cool on a rack. When cool, liberally sprinkle with the chocolate curls.

# CHERRY STRUDEL

—

THE AUSTRIAN CLASSIC SHOULD BE SERVED WITH A CUP OF BLACK COFFEE TOPPED WITH
WHIPPED CREAM.

**SERVES 8**

*2 cups fresh bread crumbs*
*¾ cup (1½ sticks) butter, melted*
*1 cup sugar*
*1 tablespoon ground cinnamon*
*1 teaspoon grated lemon rind*
*4 cups sour cherries, pitted*
*8 sheets phyllo pastry*
*confectioners' sugar, for dusting*
*whipped cream, for serving*

 Lightly fry the bread crumbs in 5 tablespoons of the butter until golden. Set aside to cool.

In a large mixing bowl, toss together the sugar, cinnamon, and lemon rind.

Stir in the cherries.

Preheat the oven to 375°F. Grease a baking sheet with a little butter.

Carefully unfold the phyllo sheets. Keep the unused sheets covered with wax paper. Lift off one sheet, place on a flat surface lined with wax paper. Brush the pastry with melted butter. Sprinkle bread crumbs evenly over the surface, using about ¼ cup of crumbs.

Lay a second sheet of phyllo on top, brush with butter and sprinkle with crumbs. Continue until you have a stack of 8 buttered sheets.

Spoon the cherry mixture on to the bottom edge of the strip. Starting at the cherry-filled end, carefully roll up the dough as for a jelly roll. Use the wax paper to help flip the strudel on to the baking sheet, seam-side down.

Carefully fold under the ends to seal in the fruit. Brush the top with any remaining butter.

Bake the strudel for 45 minutes. Let cool slightly. Using a small sieve, dust with a fine layer of confectioners' sugar. Serve with whipped cream.

# COUNTRY BREAD

—

**MAKES 2 LOAVES**

*2½ cups whole-wheat flour*

*2½ cups all-purpose flour*

*1 cup strong flour*

*4 teaspoons salt*

*4 tablespoons butter, at room temperature*

*2 cups lukewarm milk.*

**FOR THE STARTER**

*1 package active dry yeast*

*1 cup lukewarm water*

*1 cup all-purpose flour*

*¼ teaspoon sugar*

For the starter, combine the yeast, water, flour, and sugar in a bowl and stir with a fork. Cover and leave in a warm place for 2-3 hours, or leave overnight in a cool place.

Place the flours, salt, and butter in a food processor or blender and process until blended, 1-2 minutes.

Stir together the milk and starter, then slowly pour into the processor, with the motor running, until the mixture forms a dough. If

necessary, add more water. Alternatively, the dough can be mixed by hand. Transfer to a floured surface and knead until smooth and elastic.

Place the dough in an ungreased bowl, cover with a plastic bag, and leave to rise in a warm place until doubled in volume, approximately 1½ hours.

Transfer to a floured surface and knead briefly. Return to the bowl and leave to rise until tripled in volume, about 1½ hours.

Divide the dough in half. Cut off one-third of the dough from each half and shape into balls. Shape the larger remaining portion of each half into balls. Grease a baking sheet.

For each loaf, top the large ball with the small ball and press the center with the handle of a wooden spoon to secure. Slash the top, cover with a plastic bag, and leave to rise.

Preheat the oven to 400°F. Dust the dough with whole-wheat flour and bake until the bottom sounds hollow when tapped, 45-50 minutes. Cool on a rack.

# BRAIDED LOAF

SERVE THIS LOAF AT BREAKFAST WITH A VARIETY OF JAMS AND HONEY. IF THERE IS ANY LEFT
OVER IT MAKES WONDERFUL FRENCH TOAST A DAY LATER.

**MAKES 1 LOAF**

*1 package active dry yeast*

*1 teaspoon honey*

*1 cup lukewarm milk*

*4 tablespoons butter, melted*

*3 cups flour*

*1 teaspoon salt*

*1 egg, lightly beaten*

*1 egg yolk beaten with 1 teaspoon milk, for glazing*

Combine the yeast, honey, milk, and butter, stir, and leave for 15 minutes to dissolve.

In a large bowl, mix together the flour and salt. Make a well in the center and add the yeast mixture and egg. With a wooden spoon, stir from the center, incorporating flour with each turn, to obtain a rough dough.

Transfer to a floured surface and knead until smooth and elastic. Place in a clean bowl, cover, and leave to rise in a warm place until doubled in volume, about 1½ hours.

Grease a baking sheet. Punch down the dough and divide into three equal pieces. Roll to shape each piece into a long thin strip.

Begin braiding from the center strip, tucking in the ends (see left). Cover loosely and leave to rise in a warm place for 30 minutes.

Preheat the oven to 375°F. Place the bread in a cool place while oven heats. Brush with the glaze and bake until golden, 40-45 minutes. Set on a rack to cool completely.

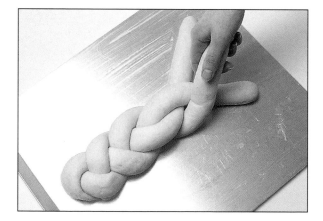

---

**COOK'S TIP**

TO MAKE THE LOAF LOOK FATTER IN THE CENTER,
STRETCH THE END STRANDS TO ACCENTUATE THE TAPER.

# PUMPKIN SPICE BREAD

—

THIS BREAD HAS A WARM AND EARTHY TASTE THAT CAPTURES THE ESSENCE OF AUTUMN. A PAT OF SWEET BUTTER AND A MUG OF CIDER ARE ALL YOU NEED AS ACCOMPANIMENTS.

42

**MAKES 1 LOAF**

*2 packages active dry yeast*

*1 cup lukewarm water*

*2 teaspoons ground cinnamon*

*1 teaspoon ground ginger*

*1 teaspoon ground allspice*

*¼ teaspoon ground cloves*

*1 teaspoon salt*

*½ cup instant nonfat dry milk*

*1 cup cooked or canned pumpkin*

*1¼ cups sugar*

*½ cup (1 stick) butter, melted*

*5½ cups flour*

*½ cup pecans, finely chopped*

In the bowl of an electric mixer, combine the yeast and water, stir, and leave for 15 minutes to dissolve. In another bowl, mix the spices together and set aside.

To the yeast, add the salt, milk, pumpkin, ½ cup of the sugar, 3 tablespoons butter, 2 teaspoons of the spice mixture, and 2 cups of the flour.

With the dough hook, mix on quite a low speed until blended together. Gradually add the remaining flour and mix on medium speed until a rough dough is formed. Alternatively, mix by hand.

Transfer to a floured surface and knead until smooth. Place in a bowl, cover, and leave to rise in a warm place until doubled, 1-1½ hours.

Punch down and knead briefly. Divide the dough into thirds. Roll each third into an 18-inch long rope. Cut each rope into 18 equal pieces, then roll into balls.

Grease a 10-inch tube pan. Stir the remaining sugar into the remaining spice mixture. Roll the balls in the remaining melted butter, then in the sugar and spice mixture.

Place 18 balls in the pan and sprinkle over half the pecans. Add the remaining balls, staggering the rows and sprinkle over the remaining chopped pecans. Cover with a plastic bag and leave to rise in a warm place until almost doubled, about 45 minutes.

Preheat the oven to 350°F. Bake for 55 minutes. Cool for 20 minutes, then unmold.

Serve warm.

# CHEESE BREAD

—

USE ONE OF THE MANY DELICIOUS VARIETIES OF CHEDDAR CHEESE AVAILABLE TODAY.
FOR A SPICY VERSION ADD A PINCH OF RED PEPPER FLAKES TO THE FLOUR.

44

**MAKES 1 LOAF**

*1 package active dry yeast*

*1 cup lukewarm milk*

*2 tablespoons butter*

*3 cups flour*

*2 teaspoons salt*

*1 cup grated sharp cheddar cheese*

Combine the yeast and milk, stir, and leave for 15 minutes to dissolve.

Over a low heat, melt the butter, let cool, and add to the yeast mixture.

Mix the flour and salt together in a large bowl.

Make a deep well in the center of the flour and salt and pour in the yeast mixture.

With a wooden spoon, stir from the center, incorporating flour with each turn, to obtain a rough dough. If the dough seems too dry, add 2-3 tablespoons water.

Transfer to a floured surface and knead until smooth and elastic. Return to the bowl, cover, and leave to rise in a warm place until doubled in volume, about 2-3 hours.

Grease a 9- x 5-inch bread pan with a little butter. Punch down the dough with your fist. Knead in the cheese (see left), distributing it as evenly as possible.

Twist the dough, form into a loaf shape and place in the pan, tucking the ends under. Leave in a warm place until the dough rises above the rim of the pan.

Preheat the oven to 400°F. Bake for 15 minutes, then lower the heat to 375°F and bake until the bottom sounds hollow when tapped, about 30 minutes more. Cool on a rack.

# CARROT CAKE WITH MAPLE BUTTER FROSTING

THIS POPULAR AMERICAN CAKE HAS A DENSE CHEWY TEXTURE AND IS DELICIOUS WITH PIPING HOT COFFEE.

**SERVES 12**

46

1 pound carrots, peeled

1½ cups flour

2 teaspoons baking powder

½ teaspoon baking soda

1 teaspoon salt

2 teaspoons ground cinnamon

4 eggs

2 teaspoons vanilla extract

1 cup dark brown sugar, firmly packed

½ cup granulated sugar

1¼ cups sunflower oil

1 cup walnuts, finely chopped

½ cup raisins

walnut halves, for decorating (optional)

**FOR THE FROSTING**

6 tablespoons unsalted butter, at room temperature

3 cups confectioners' sugar

¼ cup maple syrup

Preheat the oven to 350°F. Line an 11- x 8-inch rectangular baking pan with wax paper and grease with a little butter.

Grate the carrots and set aside.

Sift the flour, baking powder, baking soda, salt, and cinnamon into a bowl. Set aside.

With an electric mixer, beat the eggs until blended. Add the vanilla, sugars, and oil; beat to incorporate. Add the dry ingredients, in 3 batches, folding in well after each addition.

Add the carrots, walnuts, and raisins and fold in. Pour the batter into the prepared pan and bake until the cake springs back when touched lightly, 40-45 minutes. Let stand 10 minutes, then unmold and transfer to a rack.

For the frosting, cream the butter with half the sugar until soft. Add the syrup, then beat in the remaining sugar until blended.

Spread the frosting over the top of the cake. Using a metal spatula, make decorative ridges across the top. Cut into squares. Decorate with walnut halves, if wished.

---

**COOK'S TIP**

IF PREFERRED, USE THE MORE TRADITIONAL CREAM CHEESE ICING FOR THE TOP OF THE CAKE.

# PLUM CRUMBCAKE

—

FOR SPECIAL BREAKFASTS THIS MOIST FRUIT COFFEE CAKE IS A MUST. SERVE WITH A BOUQUET OF FLAVORED YOGURTS FOR A COLORFUL AND HEALTHY MEAL.

48

**SERVES 8-10**

⅔ cup (10 ⅔ tablespoons) butter or margarine, at
    room temperature

⅔ cup granulated sugar

4 eggs, at room temperature

1½ teaspoons vanilla extract

1¼ cups flour

1 teaspoon baking powder

1½ pounds purple plums, halved and pitted

**FOR THE TOPPING**

1 cup flour

⅔ cup light brown sugar, firmly packed

1½ teaspoons ground cinnamon

6 tablespoons butter, cut in pieces

Preheat the oven to 350°F.

For the topping, combine the flour, light brown sugar, and cinnamon in a bowl. Add the butter and work the mixture lightly with your fingertips until it resembles coarse crumbs. Set aside. Line a  10- x 2-inch round cake pan with wax paper and grease.

Cream the butter or margarine and granulated sugar until the

consistency is light and fluffy.

Beat in the eggs, 1 at a time. Stir in the vanilla.

In a bowl, sift together the flour and baking powder, then fold into the butter mixture in 3 batches.

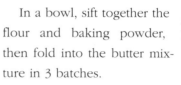

Pour the batter into the pan. Carefully arrange the plums on top.

Sprinkle the topping over the plums in an even layer.

Bake until a cake tester inserted in the center comes out clean, about 45 minutes. Take out of the oven and allow to cool in the pan.

To serve, run a knife around the inside edge and invert onto a plate. Invert again onto a serving plate so the topping is right-side up.

Serve warm, or cold the following day.

---

**VARIATION**

THIS CAKE CAN ALSO BE MADE WITH THE SAME QUANTITY OF APRICOTS, PEELED IF PREFERRED, OR PITTED CHERRIES, OR USE A MIXTURE OF FRUIT, SUCH AS RED OR YELLOW PLUMS, GREENGAGE PLUMS, AND APRICOTS.

# ANGEL FOOD CAKE

—

THIS CAKE IS AS LIGHT AS AIR. IT IS THE DARLING OF DIETERS EVERYWHERE AS IT IS
EXTREMELY LOW IN FAT BUT STILL QUALIFIES AS A BONA FIDE DESSERT. SERVE WITH SPOONFULS
OF HIGHLY COLORED FRUIT SORBETS FOR A DRAMATIC, STILL HEALTHY PRESENTATION.

**SERVES 12-14**

*1 cup sifted cake flour*

*1½ cups superfine sugar*

*1¼ cups egg whites (about 10-11 eggs)*

*1¼ teaspoons cream of tartar*

*¼ teaspoon salt*

*1 teaspoon vanilla extract*

*¼ teaspoon almond extract*

*confectioners' sugar, for dusting*

Preheat the oven to 325°F.

Sift the flour before measuring, then sift it 4
times with ½ cup of the sugar. Transfer to a bowl.

With an electric mixer, beat the egg whites until
foamy. Sift over the cream of tartar and salt and
continue to beat until they hold soft peaks when the
beaters are lifted.

Add the remaining sugar in 3 batches, beating
well after each addition. Stir in the vanilla and
almond extracts.

Add the flour mixture,
½ cup at a time, and
fold in with a large
metal spoon after
each time (see right).

Transfer to an ungreased 10-
inch tube pan and bake until
delicately browned on top,
about 1 hour.

Turn the pan upside down
onto a cake rack and let cool
for 1 hour. If the cake does not
unmold, run a spatula around the edge to loosen it.
Invert on a serving plate.

When cool, lay a star-shaped template on top of
the cake, sift over confectioners' sugar, and lift off.

# MARBLED CHEESECAKE

—

THIS RECIPE COMBINES THE FAVORITE INGREDIENTS OF TWO POWERFUL DESSERT FACTIONS:
CHOCOLATE FANATICS AND CHEESECAKE LOVERS. THE COMBINATION IS INCREDIBLE.

**SERVES 10**

*½ cup unsweetened cocoa powder*

*5 tablespoons hot water*

*2 pounds cream cheese, at room temperature*

*1 cup sugar*

*4 eggs*

*1 teaspoon vanilla extract*

*½ cup graham cracker crumbs*

Preheat the oven to 350°F. Line an 8- x 3-inch cake pan with wax paper and grease.

Sift the cocoa powder into a bowl. Pour over the hot water and stir to dissolve. Set aside.

With an electric mixer, beat the cheese until smooth and creamy. Add the sugar and beat to incorporate. Beat in the eggs, one at a time. Do not overmix.

Divide the mixture evenly between 2 bowls. Stir the chocolate mixture into one, then add the vanilla to the remaining mixture.

Pour a cupful of the plain mixture into the center of the pan; it will spread out into an even layer. Slowly pour over a cupful of chocolate mixture in the center.

Repeat alternating cupfuls of the batters in a circular pattern until both are used up (see below).

Set the cake pan in a larger baking pan and pour in hot water to come 1½ inches up the sides of the cake pan.

Bake until the top of the cake is golden, about 1½ hours. It will rise during baking but will sink later. Let cool in the pan on a rack.

To unmold, run a knife around the inside edge. Place a flat plate, bottom-side up, over the pan and invert onto the plate.

Sprinkle the crumbs evenly over the base, gently place another plate over the crumbs, and invert again. Cover and refrigerate for at least 3 hours, or overnight. To serve, cut in slices with a sharp knife dipped in hot water.

# RICH CHOCOLATE PECAN CAKE

—

THIS IS THE AMERICAN ANSWER TO VIENNESE SACHERTORTE. CHOCOHOLICS
WILL FALL ON THEIR KNEES AND THANK YOU FOR MAKING IT.

**SERVES 10**

*1 cup (2 sticks) butter*

*8 1-ounce squares semisweet chocolate*

*1 cup unsweetened cocoa powder*

*1½ cups sugar*

*6 eggs*

*⅓ cup brandy or cognac*

*2 cups pecans, finely chopped*

**FOR THE GLAZE**

*4 tablespoons butter*

*5 1-ounce squares bittersweet chocolate*

*2 tablespoons milk*

*1 teaspoon vanilla extract*

Preheat the oven to 350°F. Line a 9- x 2-inch round cake pan with wax paper and grease.

Melt the butter and chocolate together in the top of a double boiler, or in a heatproof bowl set over hot water. Set aside to cool.

Sift the cocoa into a bowl. Add the sugar and eggs and stir until just combined. Pour in the melted chocolate mixture and brandy or cognac.

Fold in three-quarters of the pecans, then pour the batter into the prepared pan.

Set the pan inside a large pan and pour 1 inch of hot water into the outer pan. Bake until the cake is firm to the touch, about 45 minutes. Let stand 15 minutes, then unmold and place on a cooling rack.

Wrap the cake in wax paper and refrigerate for at least 6 hours.

For the glaze, combine the butter, chocolate, milk, and vanilla in the top of a double boiler or in a heatproof bowl set over hot water, until melted.

Place a piece of wax paper under the cake, then drizzle spoonfuls of glaze along the edge, allowing it to coat the sides. Pour the rest on top of the cake.

Cover the sides of the cake with the remaining pecans, gently pressing them on with the palm of your hand (see above).

# RASPBERRY-HAZELNUT MERINGUE CAKE

—

THIS SHOWSTOPPER COMBINES THE CRUNCH OF MERINGUE AND NUTS WITH SMOOTH AND TART
FRUIT. IT TASTES AS GOOD AS IT LOOKS.

**SERVES 8**

*1 cup hazelnuts*
*4 egg whites*
*⅛ teaspoon salt*
*1 cup sugar*
*½ teaspoon vanilla extract*

**FOR THE FILLING**

*1¼ cups whipping cream*
*1½ pounds raspberries, about 3 pints*

Preheat the oven to 350°F. Line the bottom of 2 8-inch cake pans with wax paper and lightly grease with a little butter.

Spread the hazelnuts on a baking sheet and bake until lightly toasted, about 8 minutes. Allow to cool slightly.

Rub the hazelnuts vigorously in a clean dish towel to remove most of the skins.

Grind the nuts in a food processor, blender, or nut grinder until they are the consistency of coarse sand, only a few seconds.

Reduce the oven heat to 300°F.

With an electric mixer, beat the egg whites and salt until they hold stiff peaks. Beat in 2 tablespoons of the sugar, then fold in the remaining sugar, a few tablespoons at a time, with a rubber spatula. Fold in the vanilla and the hazelnuts.

Divide the batter between the prepared pans and spread level.

Bake for 1¼ hours. If the meringues brown too quickly, protect with a sheet of foil. Let stand 5 minutes, then carefully run a knife around the inside edge  of the pans to loosen. Transfer the meringues to a rack to cool.

For the filling, whip the cream just until firm.

Spread half the cream in an even layer on one meringue round and top with half the raspberries.

Top with the other meringue round. Spread the remaining cream on top and arrange the remaining raspberries over the cream. Refrigerate for 1 hour to facilitate cutting.

---

**COOK'S TIP**

WHEN GRINDING NUTS, BE CAREFUL NOT TO OVERDO IT.
CHECK THE CONSISTENCY A FEW SECONDS AT A TIME.

# SOUR CREAM STREUSEL COFFEE CAKE

—

THIS CRUMBLY, SWEET COFFEE CAKE LAYERED WITH CINNAMON AND NUTS IS THE QUINTESSENTIAL BREAKFAST TREAT. ONCE YOU HAVE HAD HOMEMADE YOU'LL NEVER BUY ANOTHER COMMERCIALLY PREPARED CAKE.

58

### SERVES 12-14

½ cup (1 stick) butter, at room temperature

⅔ cup granulated sugar

3 eggs, at room temperature

1½ cups flour

1 teaspoon baking soda

1 teaspoon baking powder

1 cup sour cream

### FOR THE TOPPING

1 cup dark brown sugar, firmly packed

2 teaspoons ground cinnamon

1 cup walnuts, finely chopped

4 tablespoons cold butter, cut in pieces

Preheat the oven to 350°F. Line the bottom of a 9-inch square cake pan with wax paper and grease.

For the topping, place the brown sugar, cinnamon, and walnuts in a bowl. Mix in thoroughly with your fingertips, then add the butter and continue working with your fingertips until the mixture resembles coarse crumbs.

To make the cake, cream the butter with an electric mixer until soft. Add the sugar and continue beating until the mixture is light and fluffy.

Add the eggs, 1 at a time, beating well after each addition.

In another bowl, sift the flour, baking soda, and baking powder together 3 times to capture plenty of air.

Fold the dry ingredients into the butter mixture in 3 batches, alternating with the sour cream. Fold until blended after each addition.

Pour half of the batter into the prepared pan and sprinkle over half of the walnut topping mixture.

Pour the remaining batter on top and sprinkle over the remaining walnut mixture.

Bake until browned, 60-70 minutes. Allow to stand for 5 minutes, then unmold and transfer to a cooling rack.

---

### COOK'S TIP

THE SECRET OF A GOOD CAKE IS THE MORE YOU BEAT, THE BETTER THE CAKE WILL BE. WHEN SUFFICIENTLY CREAMED, THE MIXTURE SHOULD BE SOFT ENOUGH TO FALL FROM THE WHISK AND BE LIGHTER IN COLOR.

# ORANGE WALNUT ROLL

—

**SERVES 8**

*4 eggs, separated*
*½ cup sugar*
*1 cup walnuts, chopped very finely*
*⅛ teaspoon cream of tartar*
*⅛ teaspoon salt*
*confectioners' sugar, for dusting*

**FOR THE FILLING**

*1¼ cups whipping cream*
*1 tablespoon granulated sugar*
*grated rind of 1 orange*
*1 tablespoon orange liqueur, such as Grand*
*  Marnier*

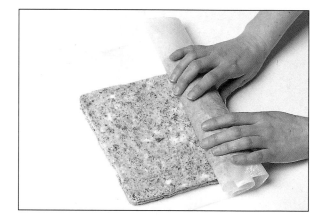

 Preheat the oven to 350°F. Line a 12- x 9½-inch jelly roll pan with greased wax paper.

With an electric mixer, beat the egg yolks and sugar until thick.

Stir in the walnuts.

In another bowl, beat the egg whites with the cream of tartar and salt until they hold stiff peaks. Fold gently but thoroughly into the walnut mixture.

Pour the batter into the prepared pan and spread level with a spatula. Bake for 15 minutes.

Run a knife along the inside edge to loosen, then invert the cake onto a sheet of wax paper that has been dusted with confectioners' sugar.

Peel off the baking paper. Roll up the cake while it is still warm with the help of the sugared paper (see above). Set aside to cool.

For the filling, whip the cream until it holds soft peaks. Stir together the granulated sugar and orange rind, then fold into the whipped cream. Add the liqueur.

Gently unroll the cake. Spread the inside with a layer of orange whipped cream, then re-roll. Keep refrigerated until ready to serve. Dust the top with confectioners' sugar just before serving.

# GINGERBREAD

—

IS THERE ANYTHING AS COMFORTING AS A SQUARE OF GINGERBREAD WARM FROM THE OVEN?
IF YOU SERVE IT AS A DESSERT, WHIPPED CREAM OR LEMON SAUCE MAKES AN ELEGANT TOPPING.

**SERVES 8-10**

*1 tablespoon vinegar*

*¾ cup milk*

*1½ cups flour*

*2 teaspoons baking powder*

*¼ teaspoon baking soda*

*½ teaspoon salt*

*2 teaspoons ground ginger*

*1 teaspoon ground cinnamon*

*¼ teaspoon ground cloves*

*½ cup (1 stick) butter, at room temperature*

*½ cup sugar*

*1 egg, at room temperature*

*¾ cup molasses*

*whipped cream, for serving*

*chopped stem ginger, for decorating*

Preheat the oven to 350°F. Line the bottom of an 8-inch square cake pan with wax paper and grease the paper and pan sides.

Add the vinegar to the milk and set aside. It will curdle.

In another mixing bowl, sift all the dry ingredients together three times and set aside.

With an electric mixer, cream the butter and sugar until light and fluffy. Beat in the egg until well combined.

Stir in the molasses (see above).

Fold in the dry ingredients in 4 batches, alternating with the curdled milk. It is much easier to handle this way. Take care to mix only enough of the curdled milk to blend.

Pour into the prepared pan and bake until firm, approximately 45-50 minutes. Cut into squares and serve warm, with whipped cream.

Decorate with the stem ginger.

# INDEX

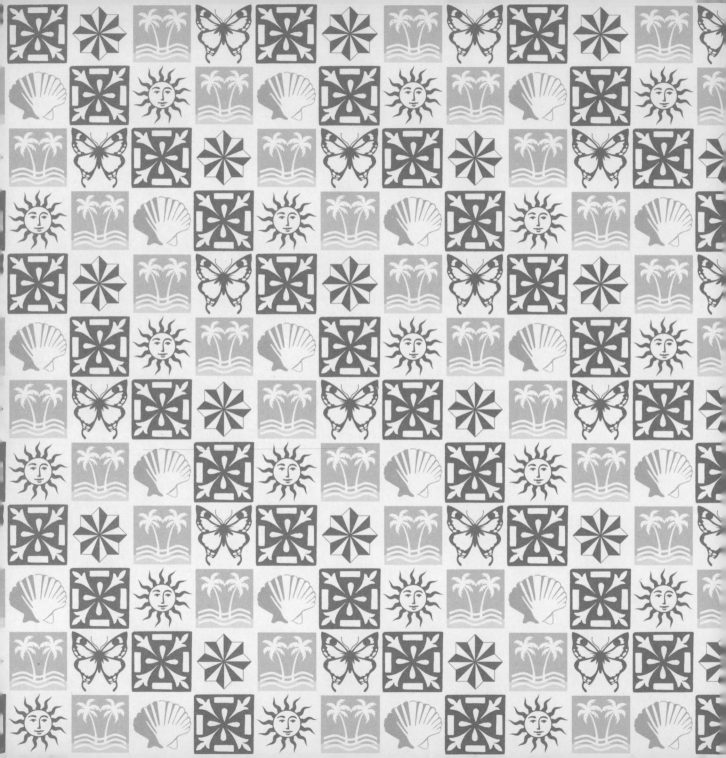